796.939
Hil   Hile, Lori
           The science of snowboarding

FOREST PARK PUBLIC LIBRARY

THE SCIENCE OF SPEED

THE SCIENCE OF
SNOWBOARDING

BY LORI HILE

CONSULTANT:
PAUL OHMANN, PH.D
ASSOCIATE PROFESSOR AND CHAIR OF PHYSICS
UNIVERSITY OF ST. THOMAS, MINNESOTA

CAPSTONE PRESS
a capstone imprint

Velocity Books are published by Capstone Press,
1710 Roe Crest Drive, North Mankato, Minnesota 56003
www.capstonepub.com

Library of Congress Cataloging-in-Publication Data
Hile, Lori, author.
The science of snowboarding / by Lori Hile.
     pages cm.—(Velocity—the science of speed)
     Summary: "Describes the science concepts involved in snowboarding"—Provided by
publisher.
     Audience: 10–14.
     Audience: Grades 4 to 6.
     Includes bibliographical references and index.
     ISBN 978-1-4765-3911-9 (library binding)
     ISBN 978-1-4765-5194-4 (pbk.)
     ISBN 978-1-4765-6059-5 (ebook PDF)
     1. Snowboarding—Juvenile literature. I. Title. II. Series: Velocity (Capstone Press)
GV857.S57H55 2014
     796.939—dc23   2013026810

Editorial Credits
Adrian Vigliano, editor; Kyle Grenz, designer; Laura Manthe, production specialist

Photo Credits
Alamy: Jef Maion, 34; Dreamstime: Emanoo, 37 (top), Lev Akhsanov, 45 (top), Maxim
Blinkov, 7, Neil Harrison, cover; fotolia: Luana R., 24-25; Getty Images: Doug Pendinger,
36-37, 40; Glow Images: All Canada Photos/Ryan Creary, 29; iStockphotos: walik, 22;
Newscom: Actionplus/Rogan Thomason, 42 (bottom), EPA/Carlo Orlandi, 10-11, EPA/Jim
Hollander, 16-17, Getty Images/AFP/Don Emmert, 38-39, Icon SMI/Bob Frid, 41, imago
sportfotodienst, 6, 14, ZUMA Press /Steve Boyle, 33; Shutterstock: Alex Emanuel Koch, 20
(bottom), Andrew Arseev, 29 (top), Ben Heyes, 12-13, Brendan Howard, 21 (bottom), Brian
Finestone, 21 (top), dotshock, 8-9, fotographic1980, (background, throughout), Jean-Francois
Rivard, 44-45 (bottom), joyfull, 11 (top), Konstantin Shishkin, 4, Magnum Johansson, 26,
Marcel Jancovic, 27, Maxim Petrichuk, 31, 43 (top), 44 (top), mountainpix, 30, NatalieJean, 5,
Pavel K, 16 (inset), Photobac, 28, S.Pytel, 32 (top), Stefan Schurr, 32 (bottom), Ventura, 18-19,
19 (top), 20 (top), Viktar Malyshchyts, 35 (inset)

Printed in the United States of America in Stevens Point, Wisconsin.
092013   007767WZS14

TABLE OF CONTENTS

Introduction:

The Need for Speed

Imagine soaring down the side of a mountain. A thin board is all that separates you from the snowy slope. Now imagine whizzing up the U-shaped wall of a **half-pipe**. Your body twists like a corkscrew as you soar into the sky above.

Snowboarders zoom down hills, carve turns, and catch enough "air" to rotate high in the sky. To accomplish these awesome feats, snowboarders rely on a board, their body, and some snow. But they also rely on science. The principles of science help snowboarders reach the heights and speeds they need to succeed.

Snowboard History

American M.J. Burchett created an early version of a snowboard in 1929. He built the board using plywood, clothesline, and horse reins. In 1965 American Sherman Poppen bound two skis together to build another early snowboard. The sport began to grow as new inventors developed more modern snowboards. But it wasn't until the late 1980s and early 1990s that snowboards were allowed at most ski resorts.

half-pipe—U-shaped ramp snowboarders use to perform jumps and other maneuvers

Chapter 1

Defying Gravity

BOARDING BASICS

Olympic Snowboard Cross gold medalist Seth Wescott crouches at the starting gate. How does he shift from standing to moving? An object or person at rest stays at rest unless a force acts on it. By pushing with his back foot, Seth creates a force that makes him move. Once an object starts moving, it will keep moving at the same **velocity** unless another force acts on it.

One of those forces is **gravity**. Gravity pulls all objects toward the center of the Earth. This pull helps snowboarders increase their speeds as they soar downhill. But gravity also slows boarders who attempt to slide up the wall of a half-pipe.

velocity—a measurement of both the speed and direction an object is moving

gravity—a force that pulls objects toward the center of Earth

There are also forces besides gravity. One is **friction**, which is created when a snowboard rubs against snow. This rubbing motion creates **resistance**, which slows the snowboard. But some friction is necessary for snowboarders. Without friction the snow's surface would become too slick, and boarders could lose control.

gravity

friction—the resistance caused by one surface moving over another
resistance—a force that opposes or slows the motion of an object;
friction is a form of resistance

USE YOUR POTENTIAL

At the top of a hill or half-pipe, boarders have potential energy, or "stored energy." As they move, this potential energy changes into **kinetic energy**. As the snowboard moves through the snow, it creates friction. The friction causes some of this kinetic energy to change to heat energy.

The heat created by friction melts some snow and creates a thin layer of water. Sometimes this water acts like a suction cup and slows down a snowboard. But the water can also reduce friction, making the snow's surface slicker and faster.

FACT

Slowing and stopping are forms of **acceleration**. Most people think of acceleration as speeding up, but actually it's any change in velocity.

kinetic energy—the energy in a moving object due to its mass and velocity; mass is the amount of material in an object

friction

Boarders face obstacles on the slopes, such as other boarders. To avoid them, boarders must learn to slow, turn, and stop. In a method called side-slipping, a boarder stands perpendicular (sideways) to the steepest part of the slope. Then the boarder digs the edge of the board deep into the slope, like a shovel's edge. This causes the slope to push back on the board, which generates friction and stops the board abruptly.

Chapter 2:

Race to the Bottom

ALPINE SNOWBOARDING

Alpine snowboarders zigzag down mountains at high speeds in races like the slalom, giant slalom, and Super G. How fast can snowboarders go? A snowboarder's speed depends on the angle of the slope, the type of snow, and the obstacles in the way. On shallow slopes, gravity has little effect on speed. But on steep slopes, boarders quickly convert potential energy to kinetic energy to propel them down faster.

FACT

Darren Powell is known as the world's fastest snowboarder. He set a world record by traveling 125 miles (201 km) per hour in May 1999.

Air resistance is another factor that affects speed. Even if a snowboarder raced straight down the slope and met with little surface friction, the boarder would face air resistance.

air resistance—the force the air puts on an object moving through it

10

At a point called **terminal velocity**, air resistance balances out gravity's pull. This balance prevents snowboarders from going any faster. By crouching down or wearing sleek gear, boarders can become more **aerodynamic**. But they cannot eliminate air resistance.

terminal velocity—the maximum velocity of a falling object limited by the friction between the object and the atmosphere
aerodynamic—shaped to move easily through the air

TURN, TURN, TURN

Although soaring straight down a slope is the fastest way down, it is also the most dangerous. To reduce the effects of gravity and navigate around objects, boarders must learn to turn.

Traversing

By zigzagging back and forth on the edge of their boards, snowboarders can control their speed. However, this method—which slows the full force of gravity—is too slow for racing boarders.

carving

Skidded Turns

Sometimes boarders rotate their shoulders and shift their weight from one leg to the other. This movement causes the board to skid sideways into a turn. But because the board's base stays flat on the snow's surface, friction slows the boarder's speed.

Carved Turns

When boarders ease left or right, the hard, metal edges of the board cut through the snow like a carving knife. Friction between metal and snow allows the board to turn. The smooth metal also helps racers retain speed.

An object only changes speed or direction when a force is applied to it. When carving, snowboarders produce this force by pushing the snowboard into the slope. But the higher the speed, the more effort is required to make the same turn.

Chapter 3

Flying Freestyle

TO THE LIMIT

In Snowboard Cross, riders race down a course filled with ramps, jumps, curved banks, and other obstacles. Snowboard Cross racers must burst out of the starting gate at the fastest possible speed. A racer's launch position often determines where he or she finishes. After launching, a rider's body has **momentum**. Heavy or fast objects in motion are harder to stop than lighter or slower ones. Boarders who are faster out of the gate have more momentum. Slow starters will find it difficult to catch up on short Snowboard Cross courses.

Snowboard Cross boarders leap off ramps at up to 60 miles (97 km) per hour. They sail through the air as far as 90 feet (27 meters) before landing. Heading into jumps, some racers crouch to keep their bodies compact and reduce air resistance. Racers know that the fastest path between two points is a straight line. So they attempt to sail through the air at the lowest, straightest possible level.

momentum—the force or speed created by movement

Some common Snowboard Cross obstacles

Kicker
a straight jump

Table
a jump with a long, flat top

Rollers
a series of small hills

Spine
an angled jump

Step-up
a jump in which the landing is at a higher point than the takeoff

landing

Banked Turn
an angled turn

FACT

At the 2010 Olympics male snowboard cross racers averaged speeds of 40 miles (64 km) per hour. Women averaged 33 miles (53 km) per hour.

TRICKING GRAVITY—THE HALF-PIPE

Freestyle snowboarders focus more on fantastic feats, such as spins, flips, jumps, and grabs, instead of fast finish times. Yet all of these amazing tricks still require speed—and plenty of it!

With six X Games wins and two Olympic gold medals, snowboarder Shaun White is the undisputed king of the half-pipe. How does science help Shaun reign?

Launch

Shaun glides straight toward the half-pipe entrance, avoiding any turns that would increase friction and slow him. The faster he zooms through the half-pipe, the higher he can fly into the air to do tricks.

GRAVITY

VELOCITY

FORCE

Shaun White flies above the half-pipe during the 2010 Vancouver Olympics.

Pump it Up

How does Shaun propel himself up a 20-foot (6-meter) half-pipe wall? At the top of the half-pipe, Shaun has potential energy. Then gravity pulls him downward. This downward movement creates kinetic energy, which pushes him to the other side. Yet to reach the top of the other side, Shaun needs more energy. So Shaun uses a technique called "pumping." He bends his knees at the bottom of the ramp, then straightens them on the way up. Pumping raises his **center of gravity** and adds more kinetic energy. The extra energy increases his speed enough to propel him to the top of the ramp. It also increases his vertical velocity, the speed with which he will sail into the air.

BIG AIR

Boarders in the Big Air competition blast into the air, twisting and turning their bodies before touching down on a massive ramp. To perform many of these amazing tricks, snowboarders must have **torque**.

Where does torque come from? Boarders must create it! Torque propels the boarder's body to rotate in the air around a vertical **axis**. This axis is like a wire running between the boarder's head and feet.

horizontal spin

vertical axis

torque—a force that causes objects to rotate
axis—straight line around which an object rotates

vertical flip

vertical axis

To create the most torque, boarders wind their bodies in the opposite direction of how they intend to spin. This technique increases the number of times that boarders are able to spin.

NOKIA
Connecting People

SLOPESTYLE

In the Slopestyle event snowboarders perform tricks as they soar down a slope lined with obstacles. Boarders slide over rails. They spin and flip off ramps and grab their boards with their hands.

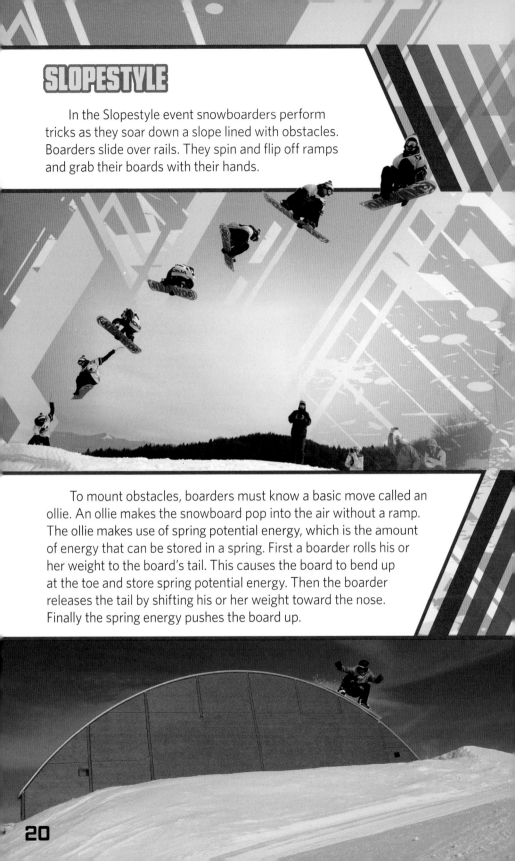

To mount obstacles, boarders must know a basic move called an ollie. An ollie makes the snowboard pop into the air without a ramp. The ollie makes use of spring potential energy, which is the amount of energy that can be stored in a spring. First a boarder rolls his or her weight to the board's tail. This causes the board to bend up at the toe and store spring potential energy. Then the boarder releases the tail by shifting his or her weight toward the nose. Finally the spring energy pushes the board up.

In a rock and roll grind, boarders ollie onto a rail, then twist their hips so that the board is perpendicular to the rail.

To stay balanced, boarders keep their boards centered over the skinny rail. And boarders keep their own center of gravity over the center of the board. Boarders sail over the rail faster than they do over snow, since the smooth rail reduces friction and increases speed.

As boarders ollie off the rail, they maintain their balance with a wide, crouching stance as they rotate the board back to straight.

Gearing Up

BOARDS, BOOTS, AND BINDINGS

Snowboard equipment consists of the 3 "Bs": the board, the boots, and the bindings. Most snowboards have a wooden core, which gives the board strength. Under the wood are layers of fiberglass, a flexible material made of plastic and glass. The board's base is a smooth plastic which helps it slide easily over the snow, reducing friction. The edges of the board are thin metal strips, which help the boarder cut through the snow. Most boards are cut in an hourglass shape, with the nose and tail wider than the middle of the board. The indentation in the center, called the sidecut, helps the boarder carve turns. The front and back tips of the board tilt up out of the snow to reduce friction.

The Benefits of Waxing a Board

Snowboarders wax their boards with a hot iron to reduce friction between the board and the snow. When boarders glide over the snow, the wax is slowly released from the board. Waxing also protects the board from marks and scratches from hard snow, ice, or other objects.

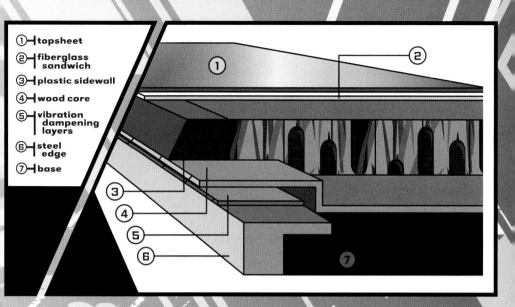

1 — topsheet
2 — fiberglass sandwich
3 — plastic sidewall
4 — wood core
5 — vibration dampening layers
6 — steel edge
7 — base

Freestyle Board

- The curved nose and tail allow boarders to ride backward as well as forward for tricks.
- Extra fiberglass allows the board to bend easily during tricks.
- The short length makes it easier to perform spins and flips.
- The broad width provides boarders a secure landing.

curved nose → ← curved tail

curved nose → ← curved tail

Racing Board

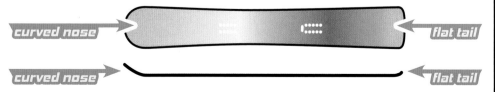

- The skinny shape lets riders quickly shift weight from one edge to the other to maintain control at high speeds.
- The narrow surface produces less friction and cuts through snow faster.
- Curved shape allows riders to carve turns without the base hitting the snow and slowing down.

curved nose → ← flat tail

curved nose → ← flat tail

DRESS FOR SUCCESS

Bindings are adjustable straps that anchor a boarder's boots to the snowboard. Bindings allow boarders to use their energy to control their board, rather than simply trying to stay on it.

To reduce air resistance, most boarders wear windproof jackets made of special fibers that block air.

When boots fit snugly, a boarder is able to transfer the kinetic energy of foot and leg movements directly to the board. If the boots are too loose, the boarder will waste kinetic energy wobbling around in the boots.

A helmet helps reduce the risk of serious head injuries. The sleek shape helps reduce air resistance.

Underneath the outer jacket, many boarders wear wool. Wool repels moisture. Wool also absorbs the sweat from a rider's body into its innermost fiber. This absorption keeps the surface of the wool and the rider's skin dry.

There are a few different types of boots. Racing boots are stiff and tight, so all foot movements quickly impact the movement of the board. Racing boots are also designed to be sleek and aerodynamic. Freestyle boots are slightly looser, allowing boarders to twist their legs and lower body to perform tricks.

FACT

Although the base of a snowboard looks smooth, it is purposely built with tiny grooves and holes on the bottom. The holes break the suction formed by melted snow.

Chapter 5:

Out in the Elements

SLIPPERY SLOPES

Snow has different textures depending on factors such as crystal shape and temperature. Each type affects a snowboard's performance differently.

Powder Snow

Powder snow forms when the temperatures in the atmosphere and on the ground are below freezing. The snowflakes are dry and powdery because they contain very little liquid.

Soft texture and a great deal of air between the flakes make powder a great landing cushion. Because of the soft, light texture, less energy is needed to carve turns, control speed, and hold an edge.

Packed Powder

Powder snow packs naturally over time. Pushing through packed snow requires less energy, so the boarder goes faster. It is also icier than powder, which improves speed.

A Day at the Slopes

With the sun's heat, temperatures can increase quite a bit as a day goes on. This increase causes snow to melt and become stickier. Wet snow gets sticky because the water molecules stick together. As a result, snowboarders' speeds can decrease.

Icy Snow

Icy snow forms when melted or rain-soaked snow freezes quickly. If the icy snow is smooth, it's very slick and ideal for fast runs.

However, carving is difficult, since boarders cannot easily dig their edges into the hard surface. Stopping and controlling the board is difficult and dangerous, since there is so little friction.

Spring Snow (also called Corn Snow)

Spring snow forms when the sun melts the top of the frozen snow base, creating a thin, soft, wet layer. The snow crystals are rounded and loose. They are also large—about the size of corn kernels.

Carves and skidded turns require little effort, since the snow is so soft. The soft snow also makes falls less painful. And its smooth surface promotes speed.

Slush

Slush forms when the sun begins melting spring snow. After repeated thawing and refreezing, delicate snowflake structures break down. As the crystals break down, they change into large, heavy grains.

Heavy, wet snow sticks to the bottom of the snowboard, preventing air from flowing underneath. The lack of air sucks the snowboard to the snow so it cannot slide easily.

AT THE SLOPES

Snowboarders in all events must adjust to ever-changing weather conditions.

Sunny Weather

This is an ideal condition for snowboarding. But snowboarders should wear sunglasses for safety. Since the color white reflects light, snow reflects the sun's rays. Extended exposure to this reflected sunlight can result in a temporary decrease in vision called snow blindness.

Whiteout

In whiteout conditions from a storm or blizzard, snowboarders can only see a few feet in front of them.

Avalanche!

The biggest danger snowboarders face are avalanches. An avalanche is a sudden flow of snow, rocks, or grass down a slope. Avalanches often happen when large, heavy snowfalls cause older, weaker layers of snow to crumble and shoot downward. Temperature changes, earthquakes, and even a boarder's own movements can also trigger avalanches.

Blizzard

With heavy, blowing snow, blizzard conditions can make it difficult for snowboarders to see. The moisture in the air is often absorbed onto the boarder's clothing. This moisture can chill the boarder, along with the heavy winds.

Chapter 6:

Boarding School

BODY BALANCE

Gravity constantly pulls us toward the center of the Earth from our center of gravity. When we stand, this point is usually located around our hips. But our center of gravity changes every time we move.

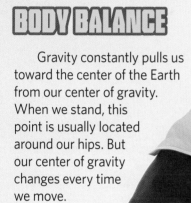

Snowboarders are constantly moving—twisting their torsos and shifting their weight. To stay balanced they must locate their ever-changing center of gravity and keep it over the board. When a boarder loses balance, the body may try to rebalance by using any available muscles. Sometimes rebalancing can cause muscle strain or injury.

Our center of gravity is located in the core. The core extends from our shoulders to our hips and includes muscles in our lower back and pelvis. Keeping the core muscles strong helps boarders maintain balance and prevent injuries.

core

quadriceps

foot

hamstring

calf

ankle

center of gravity

Boarders use hamstrings and quadriceps to push off the board. They use quadriceps and calf muscles to turn the board. Along with core muscles, strong ankle and foot muscles help boarders balance.

Snowboarders need a great deal of aerobic fitness. Aerobic activities include almost anything that makes the heart beat faster, such as jogging, running, soccer, or swimming. These activities increase blood flow and move oxygen to muscles more efficiently.

Snowboarders also benefit from anaerobic exercise, where muscles are fueled by a natural sugar called glucose. Anaerobic exercise includes activities such as sprints and weight lifting.

aerobic—involving exercise that makes the heart and lungs work harder

Anaerobic exercises tear muscles, forcing new cells to grow, which results in thicker, stronger muscle fibers. Anaerobic excercise also helps build fast-twitch muscles. Fast-twitch muscles create fuel with anaerobic activity. They fire more rapidly than slow-twitch fibers, giving athletes short bursts of energy.

Cross-training

If snowboarders only practiced snowboarding, they would overuse certain muscles. Overuse of muscles can lead to strains, sprains, and other injuries. That is why competivite snowboarders cross-train, or practice other sports in addition to snowboarding. Two-time Olympic half-pipe medalist Kelly Clark surfs and bikes to build balance and endurance. Olympic half-pipe medalist Gretchen Bleiler uses a trampoline to increase her stamina and strengthen her core. Shaun White skateboards to practice "air awareness." Air awareness is a boarder's sense of his or her surroundings.

EXTREME ENERGY

A healthy diet is also important for snowboarders. Pro boarders often eat complex **carbohydrates** before hitting the slopes. Complex carbs are found in foods such as oatmeal, granola, and whole wheat bread. Complex carbs feed fast-twitch muscles and create sustained energy. They also break down more slowly than simple carbs such as candy, cookies, or fruit. Simple carbs create a burst of energy, followed by a crash. Boarders also eat protein, found in foods such as chicken, fish, and cheese. Protein helps rebuild muscle tissue.

FACT

Competitive boarders burn between 700 and 1,260 **calories** during an hour of sustained snowboarding.

carbohydrate—a nutrient that provides energy
calorie—the measure of the amount of energy in food

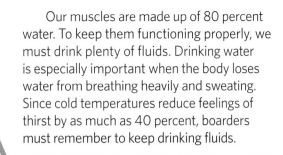

Our muscles are made up of 80 percent water. To keep them functioning properly, we must drink plenty of fluids. Drinking water is especially important when the body loses water from breathing heavily and sweating. Since cold temperatures reduce feelings of thirst by as much as 40 percent, boarders must remember to keep drinking fluids.

Snowboarder's Secret Sports Drink

After practice Olympic Snowboard Cross silver medalist Lindsey Jacobellis chugs coconut water. This sweet beverage helps rehydrate the body. Coconut water also prevents muscle cramps that can occur when the body loses too much potassium through sweat. Coconut water naturally contains about 15 times more potassium than most sports drinks. Potassium helps regulate muscles.

SNOWBOARD CROSS TRAINING

How do snowboarders prepare for the demanding sport of Snowboard Cross? Champion Nate Holland focuses on speed and balance at an indoor training center to train for the Olympics.

Out of the Gate

Nate's eyes are fixed on the indoor starting gate, his upper body forward, his hips back. As soon as the gate flops down, Nate explodes through it. He zooms down a plastic ramp into a foam pit. A computer wired to the gate measures how quickly Nate launched.

On the Course

Nate needs explosive leg power to maintain his speed. He grips the bar of a weight machine, bends down, then springs upward. He pulls his weight up with him to increase his thigh strength. Strong thighs take pressure off his knees during landings.

Air Awareness

Nate develops air awareness by bouncing high off a trampoline into a foam pit below. This also teaches him how to land in difficult positions.

Indoor Snowboard Cross training facility

The Home Stretch

To remain steady while flying over bumps, Nate practices balancing. He climbs onto a wobbling, vibrating plate that shakes his entire body while another athlete kicks the plate. Nate bends his knees to lower his center of gravity and maintain balance.

Chapter 7

Falling Down

EXTREME SPEEDS, EXTREME RISKS

New snowboarding moves are constantly invented, each more difficult and dangerous than the last. Half-pipe and ramp sizes have also increased to give boarders more "air time." And improvements in equipment allow snowboarders to fly down hills faster than ever. But faster and more difficult moves can result in more severe injuries.

Half of snowboarding injuries are caused by falling. Falls can be caused by poor visibility, icy slopes, and overused or tense muscles.

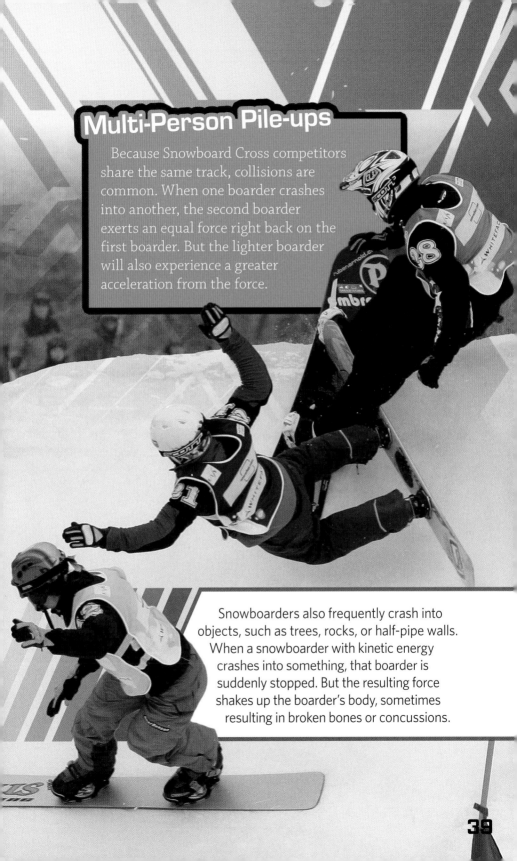

Multi-Person Pile-ups

Because Snowboard Cross competitors share the same track, collisions are common. When one boarder crashes into another, the second boarder exerts an equal force right back on the first boarder. But the lighter boarder will also experience a greater acceleration from the force.

Snowboarders also frequently crash into objects, such as trees, rocks, or half-pipe walls. When a snowboarder with kinetic energy crashes into something, that boarder is suddenly stopped. But the resulting force shakes up the boarder's body, sometimes resulting in broken bones or concussions.

COMMON INJURIES

Boarders injure their wrists more than any other body part. Wrists get injured because boarders often stick out their hands to break a fall. Boarders also break collarbones and injure necks, shoulders, backs, knees, and ankle joints.

Para-snowboarding

In 2006 a fall left British snowboarder Anna Turney paralyzed from the waist down. After years of physical therapy, Anna began competing in Paralympic competitions. She uses a mono-ski, a seat attached to a single ski. She carves turns by shifting her shoulders, arms, and core muscles instead of her legs and feet.

Anna Turney

Snowboarders are twice as likely to suffer from concussions as skiers. But helmets can prevent up to 60 percent of head and neck injuries in a snowboarding fall.

The crushable foam interior of a helmet is what protects a boarder's head. If a snowboarder falls and hits his or her head, the foam crushes and absorbs some of the impact energy. The crushing spreads the force out over a longer time. This reduces the peak impact, which means fewer head and brain injuries.

When snowboarders attempt spectacular tricks at high speeds, they often have massive crashes or falls. Concussions, caused by an impact to the head, are a common result. Athletes with mild concussions are usually treated with rest. But athletes who suffer several concussions risk problems such as depression, memory loss, and mental illness.

PREVENTING INJURIES

Snowboarders can help prevent injury by applying some scientific principles:

Boarders who bend their knees while landing jumps and tricks lower their center of gravity and create balance. Bent knees also help boarders absorb the force of landing from bumps or jumps.

When boarders land with straight legs, the leg bones above and below the knees jam together. Landing with straight legs dangerously strains knee joints. With knees bent, the thigh muscles engage and absorb some of the impact from the jump.

To reduce their chances of wrist injury, boarders can stretch their arms out like wings and slap the slope with their entire arm. This technique spreads the impact over a larger area.

Boarders finishing jumps have downward momentum toward the ground. If a boarder with downward momentum lands on a flat stretch of land, he or she will stop abruptly and risk injury. A sloping surface provides a more gradual landing. Landing in powder snow helps too. The soft, fluffy texture both slows and cushions the fall.

PUSHING THE LIMITS

Science helps us understand how boarders reach such amazing heights and speeds. Snowboarders use gravity when flying down a mountain or shooting off the wall of a half-pipe.

Snowboarders reduce friction and fly faster by waxing their boards and carving through the snow. They maximize their momentum with explosive starts out of the gate. And they increase their "air time" for spins and flips by building up speed on half-pipe walls.

Since snowboarding is a fairly young sport, boarders will push the limits of speed and height for years to come. In 2006 few people believed that a snowboarder could land back-to-back 1080s. A 1080 spin is three full rotations. Now this challenging move is standard. In 20 years moves that seem impossible today could be reality.

GLOSSARY

acceleration (ak-sel-uh-RAY-shuhn)—the change in velocity of a moving body

aerobic (ayr-OH-bik)—involving exercise that makes the heart and lungs work harder

aerodynamic (ayr-oh-dy-NA-mik)—shaped to move easily through the air

air resistance (AIR ri-ZISS-tuhnss)—the force the air puts on an object moving through it

axis (AK-sis)—straight line around which an object rotates

calorie (KA-luh-ree)—the measure of the amount of energy in food

carbohydrate (kar-boh-HYE-drate)—a nutrient that provides energy

center of gravity (SEN-tur UHV GRAV-uh-tee)—the point at which an object can balance

friction (FRIK-shuhn)—the resistance caused by one surface moving over another

gravity (GRAV-uh-tee)—a force that pulls objects toward the center of Earth

half-pipe (HAF-pipe)—U-shaped ramp snowboarders use to perform jumps and other maneuvers

kinetic energy (ki-NET-ik EN-ur-jee)—the energy in a moving object due to its mass and velocity; mass is the amount of material in an object

momentum (moh-MEN-tuhm)—the force or speed created by movement

resistance (ri-ZISS-tuhnss)—a force that opposes or slows the motion of an object; friction is a form of resistance

terminal velocity (TUR-muh-nuhl vuh-LOSS-uh-tee)—the maximum velocity of a falling object limited by the friction between the object and the atmosphere

torque (TORK)—a force that causes objects to rotate

velocity (vuh-LOSS-uh-tee)—a measurement of both the speed and direction an object is moving

READ MORE

Figorito, Marcus. *Friction and Gravity: Snowboarding Science*. New York: PowerKids Press, 2009.

Hantula, Richard. *Science at Work in Snowboarding*. New York: Marshall Cavendish Benchmark, 2012.

Schwartz, Heather E. *Snowboarding*. Detroit: Lucent Books, 2011.

INTERNET SITES

FactHound offers a safe, fun way to find Internet sites related to this book. All of the sites on FactHound have been researched by our staff.

Here's all you do:

Visit *www.facthound.com*

Enter this code: 9781476539119

INDEX